EASY PIANO

My First Classical Song Book

A TREASURY OF FAVORITE SONGS TO PLAY

T0080307

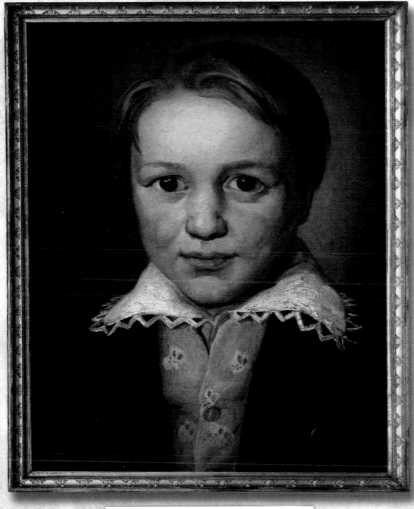

Thirteen-year-old Beethoven
Artist Unknown

Cover painting:
The Artist's Daughter at the Piano
Domingos Antonio de Sequeira

ISBN 978-1-4584-1985-9

HAL•LEONARD®
CORPORATION

7777 W. BLUEMOUND RD. P.O. BOX 13819 MILWAUKEE, WI 53213

In Australia Contact:
Hal Leonard Australia Pty. Ltd.
4 Lentara Court
Cheltenham, Victoria, 3192 Australia
Email: ausadmin@halleonard.com.au

Visit Hal Leonard Online at
www.halleonard.com

My First Classical Song Book

A TREASURY OF FAVORITE SONGS TO PLAY

CONTENTS

ARIOSO

By JOHANN SEBASTIAN BACH
(1685–1750)

Minuet in G

By JOHANN SEBASTIAN BACH
(1685–1750)

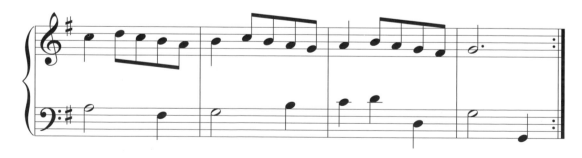

Fugue
Wassily Kandinsky

Toccata & Fugue in D Minor

By JOHANN SEBASTIAN BACH
(1685–1750)

Adagio

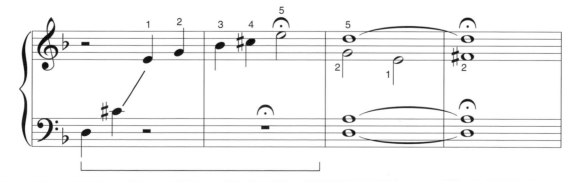

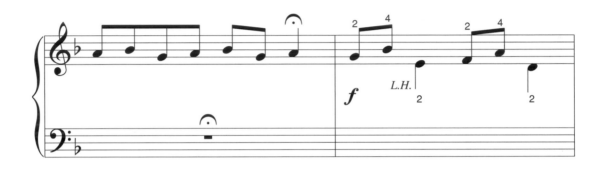

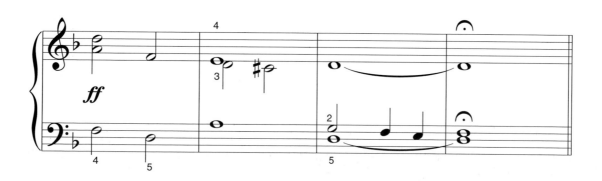

FUGUE

Für Elise

By LUDWIG VAN BEETHOVEN
(1770–1827)

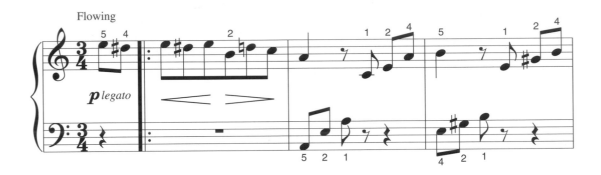

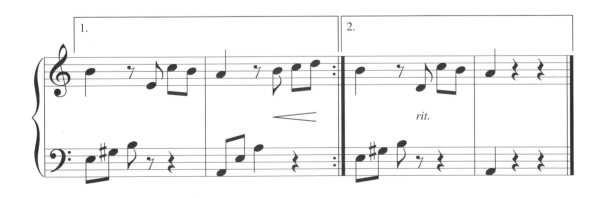

Sommer Night at Skagen Beach
Peder Severin Krøyer

Moonlight Sonata

By LUDWIG VAN BEETHOVEN
(1770–1827)

Ode to Joy

By LUDWIG VAN BEETHOVEN
(1770–1827)

Portrait of Doña Antonia Zaraté
Francisco de Goya

Habanera

By GEORGES BIZET
(1838–1875)

Allegretto quasi Andantino, in 2

mp

With pedal

mf

Hungarian Dance No. 5

By JOHANNES BRAHMS
(1833–1897)

Fast, with passion

Fine

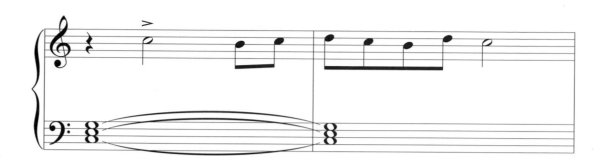

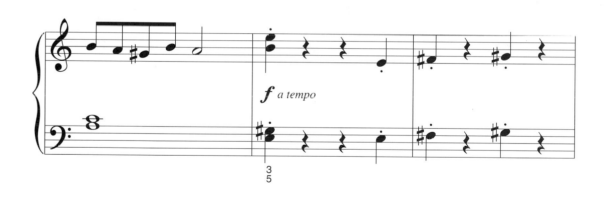

D.C. al Fine
(no repeat)

La Cuna
Berthe Morisot

Lullaby
(Cradle Song)

By JOHANNES BRAHMS
(1833–1897)

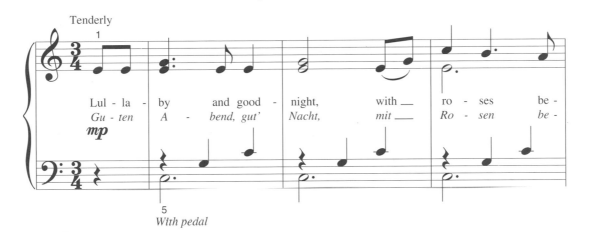

Fantasie Impromptu

By FRÉDÉRIC CHOPIN
(1810–1849)

Starry Night
Vincent van Gogh

Clair de Lune

By CLAUDE DEBUSSY
(1862–1918)

Moderately

p

With pedal

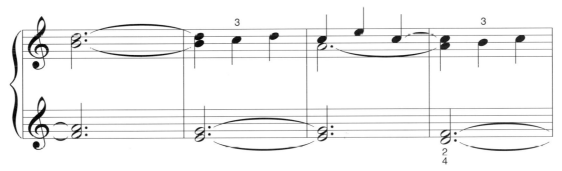

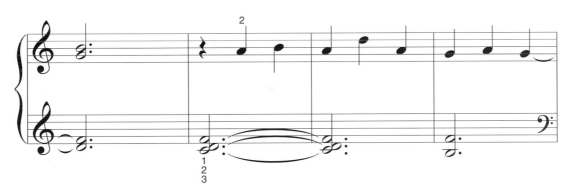

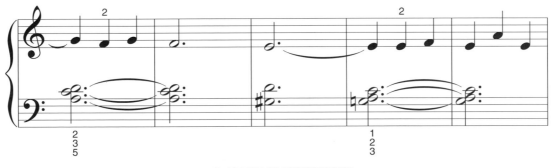

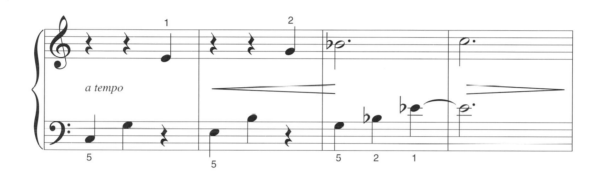

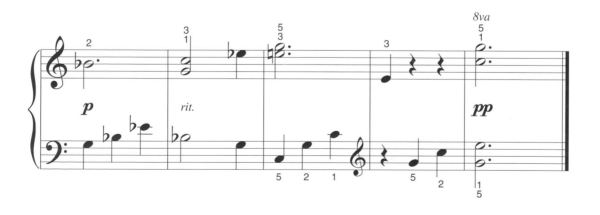

Sunlight and Shadow
Winslow Homer

REVERIE

By CLAUDE DEBUSSY
(1862–1918)

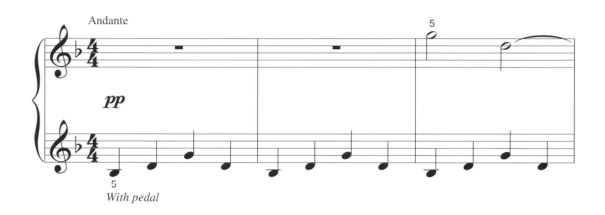

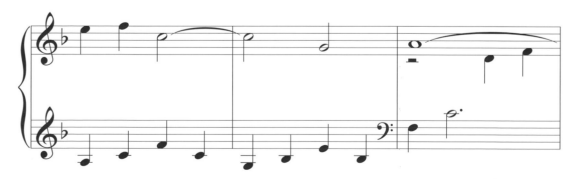

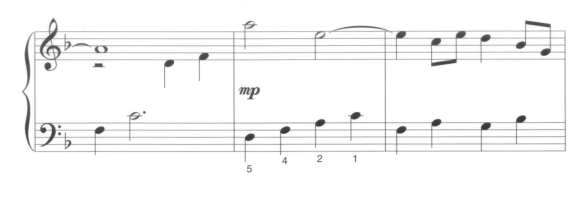

Largo from Symphony No. 9
(From the "New World")

By ANTONIN DVOŘÁK
(1841-1904)

Largo

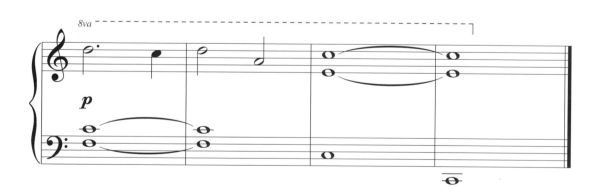

Pomp and Circumstance

By EDWARD ELGAR
(1857–1934)

The Balloon
Pal Szinyei Merse

Sicilienne

By GABRIEL FAURÉ
(1845-1924)

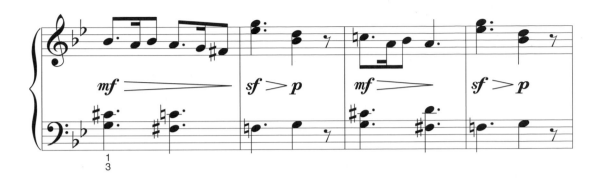

The Princess and the Trolls
John Bauer

In the Hall of the Mountain King

By EDVARD GRIEG
(1843–1907)

MORNING

By EDVARD GRIEG
(1843–1907)

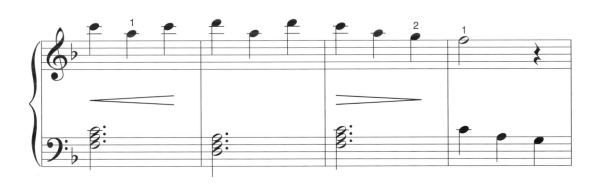

Hallelujah Chorus

By GEORGE FRIDERIC HANDEL
(1685–1759)

Majestically

Hal - le - lu - jah! Hal - le - lu - jah! Hal - le - lu - jah! Hal - le - lu - jah! Hal-

le - lu - jah! Hal - le - lu - jah! Hal - le - lu - jah! Hal - le -

lu - jah! Hal - le - lu - jah! Hal - le - lu - jah! For the Lord

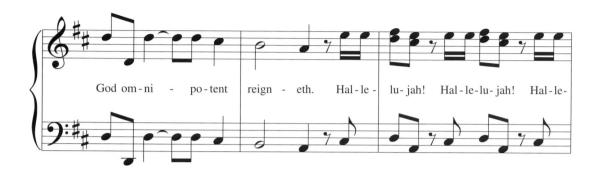

God om-ni - po-tent reign-eth. Hal-le- lu-jah! Hal-le-lu-jah! Hal-le-

lu-jah! Hal-le-lu-jah! For the Lord God om-ni - po-tent

reign-eth. Hal-le- lu-jah! Hal-le-lu-jah! Hal-le- lu-jah! Hal-le-lu-jah!

For the Lord God om-ni - po-tent reign - eth.

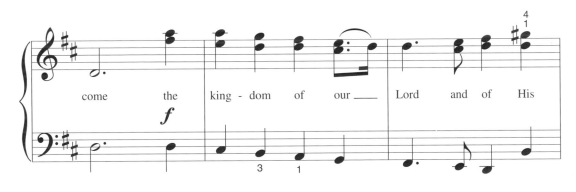

Lords, for-ev-er and ev-er. Hal-le-lu-jah! Hal-le- lu-jah! King of

Kings, for-ev-er and ev-er. Hal-le-lu-jah! Hal-le- lu-jah! And Lord of

Lords, for-ev-er and ev-er. Hal-le-lu-jah! Hal-le- lu-jah! King of

Kings, for-ev-er and ev-er. Hal-le-lu-jah! Hal-le- lu-jah! And Lord of

Lords, King of Kings and Lord _ of __ Lords. And

He shall reign for - ev - er and ev - er. King of

Kings and Lord of Lords. Hal-le-lu-jah! Hal-le-lu-jah! Hal-le-lu-jah! Hal-le-

lu - jah! Hal - le - lu - jah!

ff

Andante

By FRANZ JOSEPH HAYDN
(1732–1809)

Portrait of a Girl
Pierre-Auguste Renoir

Liebestraum
(Dream of Love)

By FRANZ LISZT
(1811–1886)

Poco allegro

To Coda ⊕

mf

Meditation

By JULES MASSENET
(1842–1912)

Moderately slow

With pedal

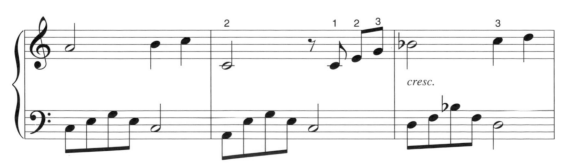

To Coda ⊕

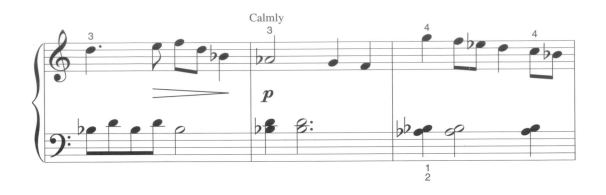

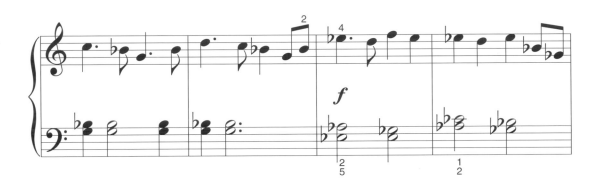

CODA

Eine Kleine Nachtmusik

By WOLFGANG AMADEUS MOZART
(1756–1791)

Moderately fast

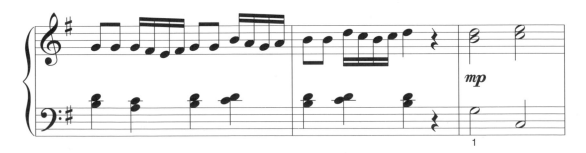

Mont Sainte-Victoire Seen from the Bibémus Quarry
Paul Cézanne

Night on Bald Mountain

By MODEST MUSSORGSKY

(1839–1881)

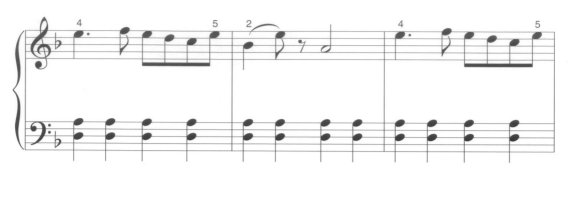

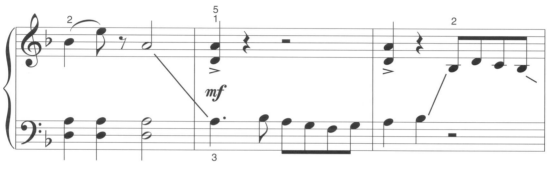

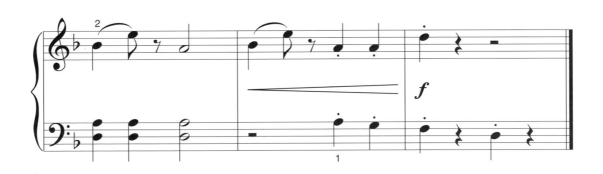

CAN CAN

By JACQUES OFFENBACH
(1819–1880)

Allegro

Canon in D

By JOHANN PACHELBEL
(1653–1706)

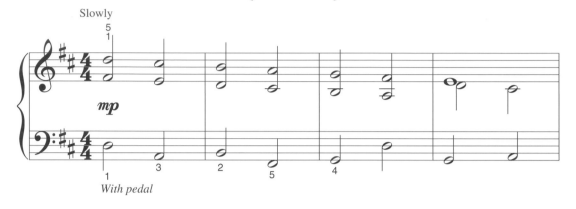

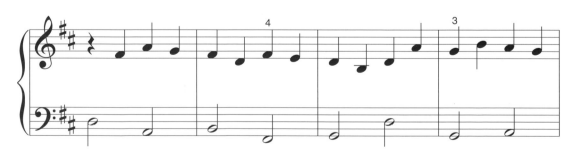

cresc.

mf

Piano Concerto No. 2, Third Movement Theme

By SERGEI RACHMANINOFF
(1873–1943)

Moderately, with expression

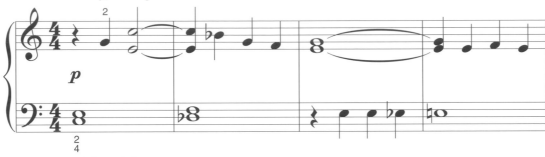

With pedal

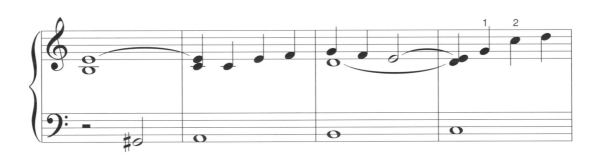

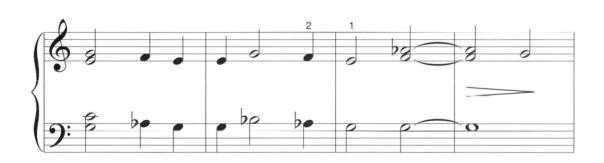

A Still Life in a Stone Niche
Cornelis de Heem

Rhapsody on a Theme of Paganini

By SERGEI RACHMANINOFF
(1873–1943)

William Tell Overture

By GIOACHINO ROSSINI
(1792–1868)

With pedal

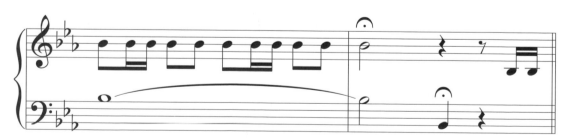

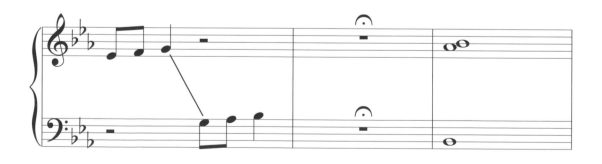

Danse Macabre
Michael Wolgemuth

Danse Macabre

By CAMILLE SAINT-SAËNS
(1835-1921)

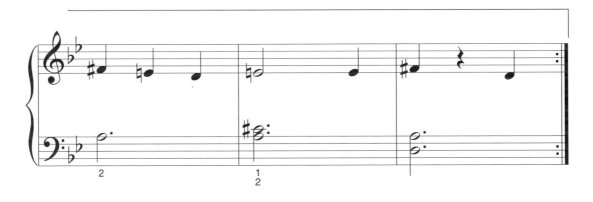

Devotion (Ave Maria)
Béla Iványi-Grünwald

Ave Maria

Traditional Latin text
Music by FRANZ SCHUBERT
(1797–1828)

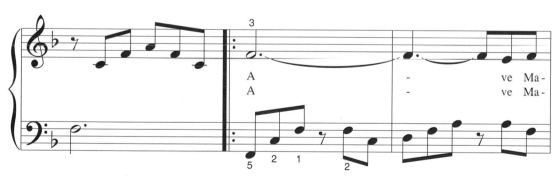

ri   -   a.
ri   -   a.

dim. al fine

pp

The Green Dancers
Edgar Degas

MARCH FROM
The Nutcracker

By PYOTR IL'YICH TCHAIKOVSKY
(1840-1893)

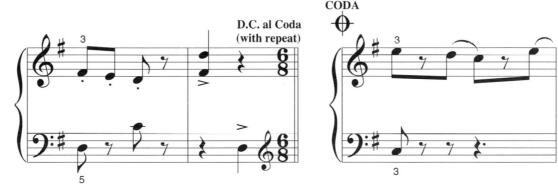

D.C. al Coda
(with repeat)

CODA

Romeo and Juliet
Frank Bernard Dicksee

Romeo and Juliet
(Love Theme)

By PYOTR IL'YICH TCHAIKOVSKY
(1840-1893)

Andante, con espressione

With pedal

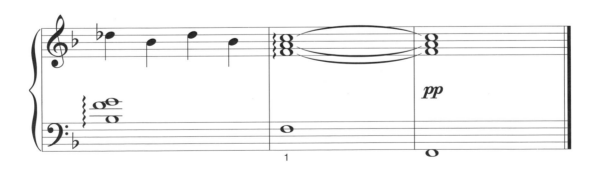

Theme from
Swan Lake

By PYOTR IL'YICH TCHAIKOVSKY
(1840-1893)

Allegro moderato

p

With pedal

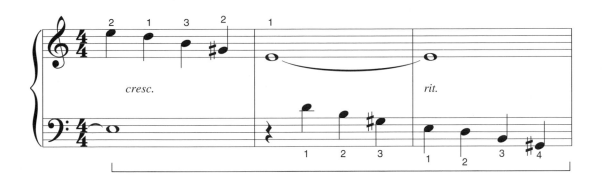

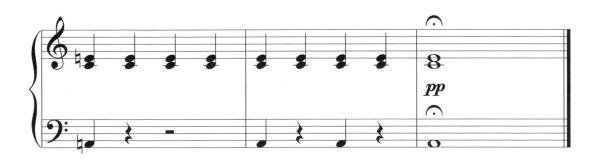

La Donna è Mobile

By GIUSEPPE VERDI
(1813–1901)

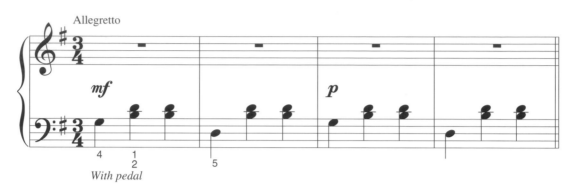

ma - bi - le   leg - gia - dro   vi - so,

in   pian - to o in   ri - so,   è   men - zo -

gne - ro.   La ___ don - na è   mo - bil

qual ___ piu - ma al   ven - to,   mu - ta   d'ac -

cen - to   e ____ di pen - sier,

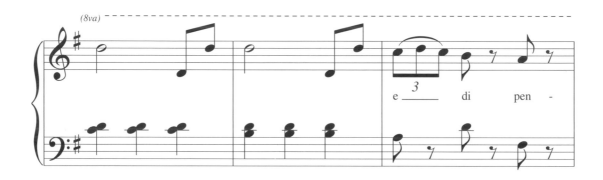

e ____ 3 di pen -

sier,   e, ____
cresc.

e ____ di ____ pen - sier.
f   *ff*